Praise for
Zen and the Art of Public School Teaching

"It's time someone told the truth about excellent teaching. John Perricone's book is mystical, practical, insightful, and remarkably refreshing for teachers struggling to serve students well in the conflicted landscape of contemporary education. His writing has given all of us in education a powerful gift with immediate use. Give it to a teacher you love. Also give it to a teacher you don't love."

—Lynn Olcott, Education Department: SUNY Cortland

"More than a book, more than a philosophy, John Perricone captures the essence of the spirit that resonates in us all, guides us in finding that spirit as it is expressed in the mission of teaching, and shows how to help young people discover the same in themselves. Perricone's words are authenticated by his own living example, as a truly powerful inspiration."

—Stan Proffitt, Corporate Educator/Leadership Consultant

"Having taught in the public school system for 34 years and reached the magical age of 56, I had started to think seriously about life after teaching when people would ask, "When are you going to retire?" Then I read *Zen and the Art of Public School Teaching*. I now realize that I've got a few more decades in me. What a pity this profoundly inspirational and perceptive book wasn't written when I started teaching."

— Gil Durham, Chemistry Teacher and Science Department Chairman, Chenango Valley CSD

John Perricone's book, *Zen and the Art of Public School Teaching*, is a book written from the heart and, like any great book, touches the heart and the mind of the reader. This book is a must read for all educators who want to be inspired, revitalized, or simply reminded of why they entered the noblest profession. It is full of wisdom, engaging anecdotes, and practical tips that will make the reader smile, both inwardly and outwardly.

— Jonathan C. Erwin, author of *The Classroom of Choice* (ASCD 2004), Faculty Member: The William Glasser Institute

ZEN AND THE ART

OF

PUBLIC SCHOOL TEACHING

BY

JOHN PERRICONE

PublishAmerica
Baltimore

First printing

Robert Fulgham's *It Was On Fire When I Lay Down on It*, Copyright 1989 by Robert Fulgham. Used by permission of Villard Books, a division of Random House, Inc.

Reprinted with permission of Simon and Schuster Adult Publishing Group from *When All You've Ever Wanted Isn't Enough* by Harold Kushner. Copyright 1986 by Kushner Enterprises, Inc.

Author's website: JohnPerricone.com

ISBN: 1-4137-6648-X
PUBLISHED BY PUBLISHAMERICA, LLLP
www.publishamerica.com
Baltimore

Printed in the United States of America

"I AM INDEBTED TO MY PARENTS FOR LIVING,
AND TO MY TEACHER FOR LIVING WELL."

– ALEXANDER III OF MACEDONIA

This book is dedicated to my parents, Frank and Josephine Perricone, who gave me life, a wonderful childhood filled with love, nurturance, and support, to my wife Vicki and my children Loren and Hannah who have given my life its deepest meaning and purpose, and to my teacher Master Hidy Ochiai whose wisdom and example inspired me to pursue the most challenging and fulfilling art of all—the art of being a teacher.

INTRODUCTION

This book is based on two assumptions. The first is that "we teach who we are," and the second is that one's philosophy of life is intimately tied to one's identity, and that it is that identity (conscious or otherwise) that ultimately dictates one's teaching style, and also that distinguishes those who find joy and passion in the teaching profession from those who find drudgery and then simply pick up a paycheck every two weeks.

This book is for those who are just beginning their careers in teaching, for those who are experienced veterans and who are still open to personal and professional growth (not mutually exclusive realities, as some often assume), and those who are thinking about becoming a teacher.

I welcome you on a journey inward, and a journey into a world, that for all its inherent frustrations offers greater rewards, meaning, and fulfillment than any other profession than I can possibly imagine.

CONTENTS

"WHAT THE TEACHER IS, IS MORE IMPORTANT
THAN WHAT HE TEACHES."
– KARL MENNINGER

CHAPTER ONE

WHO AM I?

There is probably no greater journey we will take in this life than the one we take in search of our identity (and this is true of our students as well), and so I begin this book with questions designed to heighten your personal awareness of this ever evolving path. Let me also state from the outset that I believe unequivocally that introspection cannot be forced or thrust upon someone, and therefore what you take from this reading will be intimately linked to your willingness and desire to actively participate in the exercises provided here. Please feel free to make parts of this book a writing journal. I know you've been told your entire life not to write in books, but trust me…you can run with the bulls here and let yourself be unencumbered. Write in this book. This will help you, as Socrates said, to "Know thyself" and it will help me sell more books because no one wants to read a book someone else has written in. It's becoming evident that we're already beginning to bond.

Let me begin by posing some questions that on their surface may seem to have obvious answers, but bear with me as we build toward something I hope you'll agree is rather profound: **WHEN YOU LOOK INTO A MIRROR, WHAT DO YOU SEE?**

In a civilized society, one would reasonably answer that "I see myself" or at a somewhat deeper level one might say that "I see my perception of myself." This is good. Next question: **AND AS YOU GO ABOUT YOUR DAY, WHAT PRONOUNS DO YOU USE WHEN MAKING REFERENCE TO YOURSELF?** (Again, "I" or "me" would make a lot of sense here.)

When someone says to you, "Excuse my lapse in memory, but may I ask who you are?" the average person, wanting to be polite, would likely offer up their name. And now for the hard part. If I asked you, **"WHO ARE YOU?"** and you are not allowed to use your name or any of the pronouns that you would normally use to define yourself, what would you say? (Please take a moment to think about this).

Several years ago I recall returning home from graduate school to visit my parents and as I walked into their home I could hear a woman's sobbing coming from my mother's living room. My mother greeted me in the dining room and whispered to me that her close friend had just been blindsided by the fact that her husband was leaving her. My mother, visibly shaken by this news and yet wanting to help her friend, was at a loss as to what to do. Knowing that I had had training in the mental health field, she asked me, "John, would you mind speaking with Mary? Maybe you could help her." I said that I would be happy to do my best and so Mary and I made our way into my parents' finished basement where I simply listened for three hours as this broken-hearted and decimated woman poured her heart out to me. What I most remember from that conversation some 25 years later was this comment, accompanied by trembling and tears: "John, without my husband in my life, I don't know who I am. My whole identity is wrapped around my relationship to him. Even my mail comes addressed Mrs. David…."

I drove home to my apartment in Cortland, New York, that night, and as I sat in my living room watching TV a fight broke out between the couple residing in the apartment above me. I must admit that I was in a state of ironic shock when I heard this woman screaming at the top of her lungs at her husband, "DON'T YOU UNDERSTAND? I DON'T KNOW WHO I AM!!!" Outside of my obvious concern for their anguish, I sat stupefied thinking to myself, *What are the statistical chances of my being aware of this issue of identity arising in two different couples' lives to such a degree on the exact same day?*

And so it seems apparent that the issue of "identity" is a central one in our uniquely human quest, and one that resonates and permeates every other aspect of our lives, both personally and professionally. We've heard of people falling apart amidst an *identity crisis* where they may find themselves questioning their marriages, careers, roles, or the lack of meaning or fulfillment that they are experiencing at any given point in life.

Because our identity lies at the foundation of forming relationships of any kind (marriage, business, student/teacher etc.), it seems a logical place to begin our journey inward by stopping to reflect upon who we are (or who we perceive ourselves to be) at this very moment in time.

I ask you now to do the following. I have written the words "I am…." At the bottom of this page, and I am going to ask you to do your best to fill in the 20 slots that follow with anything (and I mean anything) that you personally identify with at this point in your life. (Such as "I am a mother, a friend, shy, religious, etc.) Please do not read any further until you have done this, and be assured that this is not easy for many people.

"I am….

1.
2.
3.
4.
5.
6.
7.
8.
9.
10.
11.
12.
13.

14.
15.
16.
17.
18.
19.
20.

Please take a minute or so to reflect upon what you have written above. I'm now going to ask you to code them. Please put an:

A—next to anything on your list that describes you in terms of size, weight, color, or sex (Examples: I am a woman, tall, slim etc.) These are mostly things about you that would be visible to anyone looking at you without knowing anything else about you.

B—next to anything on your list that places you within a particular institution, organization, or club (I am a mom, PTA member, sister, provider, etc.).

C—next to any adjectives that describe ways of acting or feeling (examples: I am shy, religious, optimistic, caring etc.).

D—next to any statements that completely remove you from any particular structure or social construct (examples: I am what I am, or I am one with the cosmos).

Though there are no right or wrong responses here, I would ask you to go back and count how many of each of these letters you accumulated aside your list. If you have a majority of A statements, this simply suggests that at this point in your life, much of your identity has been derived from your perception of yourself as a physical being. People who score high in the B category are people who define much of who they are by the organizations or clubs that they belong to. For example, your identity as a Catholic, or a basketball coach (or in my case a barbershop harmony singer) may be deeply significant to you. Those who have a majority of C statements are people whose identity are very much rooted in current feelings and experience. And finally those who have a majority of D statements (this is extremely rare: in 22 years of giving this exercise to my students, only 2 scored highest in this category) are people who are defined as free-floating selves, and who are anchored in nothing but abstractions. I'm assuming that Rod Serling (the brilliant creator of the *Twilight Zone*) might have scored high in this particular rating. My experience over the years in utilizing this activity for both students and adults, is that B's and C's are most common.

Now for the hard part. Would you please go back to your list and rank order the top 5 components of your identity with #1 being the most important one on your list—the one you cannot imagine living without. Would you now do the same with the next four?

Now just when you didn't think it could get any more difficult, would you please do the following? Draw a thin line through #5 and imagine that this has been permanently removed from your identity. How much of an impact would this have on your life? Could you go on being the person you perceive yourself to be if this were taken from you? Did you indeed disappear from the world in doing this, or do you still exist, but in a lesser state of being? Would you now do the same with numbers 4, 3, 2, and finally number 1?

Who are you now? What kind of person would you be? Do you exist at all? Was the word "teacher" anywhere on your list? What does this tell you?

I hope in some small way this exercise helped you to hone your identity and sense of self, as I am more convinced than ever after 22 years in the classroom that "knowing ourselves" is the essential prerequisite to helping our students find their place in the world.

"A TEACHER AFFECTS ETERNITY;
HE CAN NEVER TELL WHERE HIS INFLUENCE STOPS."
— HENRY BROOKS ADAMS

"OUR TEACHER INTRODUCED US TO OURSELVES.
WE LEARNED WHO WE WERE AND WHAT WE WANTED TO BE.
WE WERE NO LONGER STRANGERS TO OURSELVES."
— STUDENT TRIBUTE

CHAPTER TWO

WHY AM I A TEACHER?

When I was in the ninth grade a friend invited me to a karate exhibition being given by a world-renowned karate master by the name of Master Hidy Ochiai. As I sat in the audience, I was awestruck by this man's presence. Only 5' 2" and 120 lbs., he immediately commanded the respect of this packed auditorium by demonstrations of physical and mental prowess that seemed to defy any degree of human conditioning that I had thought were possible. Two-hundred-fifty-pound men were being thrown through the air as if they were the weight of feathers. Later in his demonstration he blindfolded himself, placed an apple on the throat of a volunteer who was lying on three chairs, and proceeded to swing a razor-sharp samurai sword downward with astonishing speed slicing the apple in perfect halves, leaving the man below the apple unscathed and in perfect health. Just when I thought that nothing could come close to what I had already witnessed, he finished his demonstration by lying on a bed of nails that were piercingly sharp after which six cinderblocks were placed on his stomach and then demolished by a huge man wielding a sledge hammer with uncanny force.

The audience went silent as Mr. Ochiai calmly approached the microphone and with a huge smile on his face began to explain that what we had just witnessed was simply a metaphor for life, and that "where there is a will, there is a way." I knew in the profundity of that moment that what this little man from Japan was teaching far transcended punching and kicking, and that I had, perhaps the first time in my life, grasped the meaning of the word "potential."

Let it suffice to say that I became Mr. Ochiai's student that week, and since that day have not missed a week of training with him in thirty-two years. Though I could dedicate an entire book to the wisdom that this man has generously imparted to me (and I will speak more to that wisdom later in my writing), I want to make it clear that Mr. Ochiai is the sole reason that I became a teacher twenty-two years ago. He had such a positively profound impact on my mental, physical, and philosophical development growing up that when it came time to choose a profession, I honestly could not think of anything greater to aspire to than to teach because I, too, wanted to have the opportunity to affect others' lives in the way that he had affected mine.

My point in sharing this story is simply to highlight that everyone has a story. Every one of us was

The author's teacher,
Master Hidy Ochiai

20

drawn to this profession for a variety of reasons and motives, and I'm going to naively assume that money wasn't one of them. I shared my impetus for pursuing this vocation above and now ask you to reflect on one of the most important questions that I will raise in this book, and that question is simply: **WHY DID YOU BECOME A TEACHER?**

Please take the time in writing to reflect on who or what motivated you to pursue the teaching path. Who inspired you? What qualities did this person or persons possess that made you want to follow in their footsteps? What were your dreams for being a teacher? (Please reflect below.)

At the end of each semester, I ask my students to anonymously evaluate my course because I remind them that although they are leaving, I am staying and want to make my course the best that I possibly can for the next group of students who will fill their seats. I tell them that they are welcome to sign their evaluations, but that it's been my experience that anonymity tends to encourage greater honesty—especially if a student may feel the need to be particularly critical. As this school year was coming to a close, a young woman from my class approached me earlier in the morning and handed me her evaluation, saying, "Mr. Perricone, I wanted you to know that this was from me and hoped that you would read it before I have you for our last class." I thanked her for her kindness and proceeded to read the following:

Dear Mr. Perricone,

I wanted this evaluation to be more personal and formal than others that you might receive. I'm not even sure where to begin, but I guess I can start by saying thank you. Thank you for providing me with the most enlightening, enjoyable, and knowledgeable class that I have ever been in. The past semester has left me with an entirely new outlook on life, love, sex, and the choices that I'll be given in the future. I can't even begin to explain how wonderful a person you are. I had been so afraid that I would never find out what I wanted to do with my life, but I know now that I would like to pursue a career in health education and try with everything I've got to become as great of a teacher as you are. You stand in front of some twenty-five students five days a week, not being paid even close to what you deserve, and you do so with the most positive, exciting, and influential aura. You are single handedly the most interesting, passionate, humane person that I have encountered in my life, and I swear that I remember every story, every lesson, and every amazing piece of wisdom that you shared. I learned more about myself in these past five months than I have in my whole life. The way that I handle problems has gotten noticeably better, and I find that I have learned more from you in one semester than I did in all of my high school career. There have been so many times in the past few years of my life that I came so close to moving, but I think that I was meant to stay so that I could know the experience of your class. The way you speak of your wife, family, your karate training, your profession, experiences, family, and those who have passed away—it's truly inspiring. Thank you for all the knowledge you have blessed me with, and for playing such a huge part in helping me find my future career. I will miss you and your class greatly, and will do everything in my power to get into your elective class next year.

Jen Tallman

I could not have been more deeply humbled and touched, and though I have never shared such evaluations with anyone but my wife, I did so here to make it clear why I teach. She said more than any explanation I could muster. There is no amount of money anyone could pay me to trade this life's work for something else where "I could be making a lot more."

I hope it's evident at this point that I love my career and consider it the greatest of honors to stand before my students each day and offer up thoughts and discussions that may facilitate a process that has as its end the betterment of young peoples' lives. I left a job making four times what I make in teaching, and I have never looked back once. It is with tremendous anticipation that I look forward to the years that lie ahead.

When I was asked why I teach, it reminded me of this little saying that probably says why I do. "To laugh often and much; to win the respect of intelligent people and the affection of children; to earn the appreciation of honest critics and endure the betrayal of false friends; to appreciate beauty; to find the best in others; to leave the world a bit better, whether by a healthy child, a garden patch or a redeemed social condition; to know even one life has breathed easier because you lived. This is to have succeeded." – Author unknown

"THE MIND IS ITS OWN PLACE, AND IN AND OF ITSELF
IT CAN MAKE A HEAVEN OF HELL, OR A HELL OF HEAVEN."
– JOHN MILTON'S *PARADISE LOST*

CHAPTER THREE

DEVELOPING A PHILOSOPHY
OF LIFE AND TEACHING

Though we all have bad days, one of my pet peeves in education are teachers who consistently walk the halls with this look on their face, which in effect says, "Stay the hell away from me." My first thought upon witnessing this is "What is this really communicating to students between the lines? "Study really hard, go to college, and someday you can grow up to be a miserable human being just like me." If I were a student in this situation, my thoughts would be: "Why should I listen to anything you have to say—clearly your philosophy of life is not working."

Never in my life have I been more convinced that it is our philosophy of life that dictates our philosophy of teaching, and that it is this "philosophical identity" (or lack of same) that we envelop ourselves in each day as we walk into our classroom that ultimately distinguishes those who find joy and passion in this profession from those who find drudgery and then just pick up a paycheck two weeks later.

So the next question of ultimate relevance to your life and to your career that I ask you to ponder is this: **WHAT IS YOUR PHILOSOPHY OF LIFE AND HOW DOES IT RELATE TO YOUR TEACHING STYLE AND YOUR IDENTITY AS A TEACHER?**

I have the honor and pleasure of teaching a senior elective course that I wrote several years ago which I entitled "Personal Dynamics"—a course, that is, much like this book, heavy on introspection and looking inward to the experience of our humanity. Almost without exception, we each day sit in a circle and discuss issues relevant to our personal growth and evolution or lack of same. One of the books I ask my students to read and discuss in this course is Dr. Victor Frankl's *Man's Search for Meaning*. Frankl, a survivor of the Nazi concentration camp at Aushwitz, had, as did all who lived his horror, everything that is important to a human being stripped away from him—his family, clothing, food, dignity etc., and yet in this state of utter deprivation he found that many people huddled together, trying to find meaning in what was happening to them. He hypothesized that if people were still looking for meaning under such horrific conditions, certainly the need to find meaning in life was a major motive and common human denominator. Born of his experience he created an entire branch of psychology he coined "logotherapy." Though I cannot do justice to defining it here, the essence of his theory and practice is this: when a person can find meaning in their suffering, it ceases to be suffering. He dedicated his life and practice to helping others do just that.

For example, two couples give birth to a blind child. One couple becomes cold, embittered, and unsociable and decides to slam the door on the world. The other couple looks to each other and says "Honey, what do you say we open up a school for blind children?" Though the stressors and experience were the same, the couples chose to perceive them differently. One chose for bitterness and stagnation, the other for growth and vitality.

One could argue that it is this unique human ability to create, attach, and find meaning in our experiences that truly separates us from the animals, and what makes the human journey such a profound one. No other living thing, it appears, has this ability to "choose its perception."

SOME EXAMPLES FROM MY PERSONAL LIFE

STORY #1

For sixteen years (1979–1995), I had the honor of representing my karate Master, Mr. Hidy Ochiai, by teaching a branch of his school on the campus of SUNY Cortland. During that time, I had more than four thousand students experience the very training that had so enriched my life. One young man who had no choice but to distinguish himself was a man by the name of David Best. Though he was my student, to this day, I consider him one of the greatest teachers I have ever known.

Though I couldn't quite pin it down at the time, I knew that there was something very unique about David's temperament . He spoke to you in an extremely calm voice, and there was a focus, compassion, and empathy about him that certainly broke any stereotype that unfortunately was more than not associated with many of the young men on this campus. Though I thought of his unique character often, the logistics of my driving to this campus to teach and then leaving shortly after the class ended denied me the opportunity to "socialize" with my students. It wasn't until two years later (David was still my student) that I was at a social gathering where David and I sat down to talk, and during the course of that conversation I learned this about him. When he was sixteen, his mother died of breast cancer. When he was seventeen, his father was struck and killed by a drunk driver. Six months later, his oldest brother was killed in a freak trucking accident, and three months after that his youngest and only remaining brother took his life because of his overwhelming grief and inability to deal with it. If ever in my life I had met a man who would have been justified in slamming the door on this life and saying "To hell with this," it was David Best. But you know what he did? He took this miserable hand of cards that was dealt to him and decided this was what he had to work with. David went on to get his master's degree in psychiatric social work where he specialized in grief counseling — in helping others cope with what he had, through no choice of his own, become an expert in. I came, through learning of his history, to understand that the compassion and empathy that I had earlier observed in him were by-products of his journey—and that when he talked to you, he was totally present in that moment because he had learned, perhaps more than anyone else that I have ever encountered, that the things that we often assume are permanent in our lives (our families, friends etc.) can slip through our hands in a second, and so when he spoke to you, he did so as if there were literally no tomorrow. Again, one of the greatest teachers in my life, David is now happily married with two children and continues a fulfilling career as a social worker. Because he continued his martial art training, we see each other often.

STORY #2

My first official teaching job was in 1983 at West Middle School in Binghamton, N.Y. My principal, Mr. Muhammad Husami, was a warm, compassionate man who I had had as a science teacher when I was in the 7th grade, and again for chemisty in the 10th grade. The irony is that I hated taking his classes because of the subject matter he taught, but he was the teacher that I most often went back to visit— not because of what he taught, but rather because of who he was. He was the teacher that somehow always had time to talk when you needed him, and I remember on many occasions his choosing to eat lunch with me over taking his much deserved break in the faculty lounge. He, too, studied karate with Mr. Ochiai, and so our roots, if you will, ran deep.

Long story short. Mr. Husami leaves teaching to become a principal, and though I'd lost touch with him during my years of college and pursuing my master's degree, he happened to see my application on his superintendent's desk, and having a health position to fill he said to his superintendent, "That's who I want for the job." Our lives were once again connected.

Later that year I was attending a Christmas dinner where Muhammad was seated next to me. About halfway through our meal he leaned toward me and whispered, "John, I just wanted to let you know that I'm going in for some exploratory surgery tomorrow. I've been having spells of uncontrolled bleeding from my nasal passages and they want to figure out what's causing it." And then the bomb fell. To the shock of all that knew and loved this man, we learned that his surgery had revealed a malignant tumor the size of an orange sandwiched between his eye and his skull. He was told he had six months to put his life in order.

I remember quite vividly the sobering days that followed as we all tried to go about our days of teaching. Despite the hustle and bustle of the kids around us, those of us who were close to Muhammad felt like we were moving through quicksand. Being a fighter, Muhammad continued to work, despite surgery through the roof of his mouth and what seemed like endless radiation treatments that left him scarred and blind in one eye.

When someone is diagnosed with such a cruel illness, there is a tendency among people to want to be close to that person, and yet their inherent discomfort with not knowing what to say often keeps them at a distance. I reasoned that for all that I had been through with him, and if I was going to be any kind of friend at all, I would have to cut through my own discomfort so that I could be there for him. It was time to "have lunch" with Muhammad again. I knocked on his always opened office door, and in his now softer voice he kindly said, "Come in, John. Sit down." And there he sat—my favorite teacher, who though determined to keep working, was visibly frail, scarred, and bruised from his radiation treatments, and wearing an eyepatch to cover where his vision had once resided. I simply said, trying to mask the fear and trembling in my own voice, "How are you, Muhammad?"

And it was these words that will resonate with me for a lifetime. He leaned toward me and said, "You know what, John? I look upon my cancer as an opportunity."

"An opportunity?" I asked in a most perplexed voice.

"May I ask what you mean by that, Muhammad?"

He went on: "As an opportunity to develop aspects of my character and my humanity that I would never have had the opportunity to develop had I not faced this challenge in my life. Length of life is no longer the issue for me, but the quality of what life I have remaining is."

Muhammad went on to defy his death sentence of six months by embracing another eight years by living much as David Best did—with even greater depth, wisdom, compassion, and commitment to the sanctity of his life and the lives of his family, friends, and coworkers. To his last breath, he taught me how to better live mine.

I'm reminded in sharing this story that the Chinese character that connotes "crisis" is the same character that connotes "opportunity." I often ask my students, "Is this a crisis, or an opportunity that life is offering you?" I will forever be indebted to Muhammad for teaching me this life lesson.

Story #3

I'll keep this story short. My father, Frank Perricone, was diagnosed with a brain tumor in 1988 and died ten months later in April of 1989. During the last six months of his life, we were fortunate enough to have him enter Lourde's Hospital Hospice Program, which allowed him to stay home surrounded by his family and friends. It was through Hospice that we met my father's aide, an angel on earth by the name of Tricia Alamo. Tricia came to visit my father every day dressed as if she had just come from church, and to this day I don't know if I have ever met a woman who was so well versed in the art of communication. My father, being rather shy by nature, wasn't a big talker, but to everyone's amazement, Tricia could draw three amazing hours of dialogue from him every single day, five days a week. I think she said more to him in one three-hour session than he and I did in his entire life.

I remember on one particular day pulling Tricia off to the side and simply asking her this question: "Tricia, how do you do it? How do you continue to form deep relationships with people you know are not long for this world?" She simply smiled and said, "Well, you know, John, everyone has to make this journey across the bridge between life and death, and I consider it a great honor to be the one holding their hand." Notice she didn't say, "Hey, if I don't change their bedpans, who's going to do it?" No, instead she had a profound philosophy that enabled her to see herself as a spiritual guide, and it was this very deep sense of mission and identity that allowed her to do her very important work again and again. Tricia became such an important person in our life that I asked her if she would be a godparent to my second child. She joyfully obliged.

In each of these people we see a common thread, and that commonality was their ability to frame a philosophy of being and identity that bore meaning and fulfillment in their individual lives despite their ominous circumstances.

Robert Fulgham, author of *All I Ever Needed to Know I Learned in Kindergarden*, and *It Was On Fire When I Lay Down on It*, shares a wonderful passage in his second book about his encounters with a driver education teacher who somehow had a profound influence in the lives of his students. When I speak to educators, I often play a recording of him reading the following passage from his book because I think it speaks volumes to the theme of identity and its significance in our work as teachers.

In most American high schools there is someone who teaches driver training—the top sergeant of automotive bootcamp. It's a thankless task, a low status job about in the same league with the typing teacher as far as the faculty pecking order is concerned. The driver trainer is something of a non-person on campus. The parents of students never meet the D.T. The students see the D.T. as a necessary evil—one more adult whose bottom they must kiss in order to get something they want. It's a job that anyone with half a brain could do and anybody who wants the job doesn't have much ambition, or talent, or skill. Maybe. Nevertheless, I would like to teach driver training for awhile. It would be an honor, now that I see it the way old Mr. Perry sees it. The students call him that—old Mr. Perry. They also call him the driving master and Obie Wan Kenobie. Since the latter name refers to the wise one in the Star Wars Trilogy I asked some students the reason and they said "Take a ride and see." And so I did.

Jack Perry. Very average in appearance—not tall, or short, or fat or thin or old or young or straight or weird—

kind of generic. You'd not notice him on the street or pick him out of a police lineup for ever having done anything remarkable. He's a former Navy Chief Petty officer—retired, one wife, four kids all grown. Protestant. Tends his garden for pleasure. Likes cars and kids. And so, he's the Driver Trainer. Now it seems fair and useful to say that the conversation that follows is a reconstruction in my mind of what went on between us. What I'm sharing is the spirit of the interchange. A taciturn man, Jack Perry actually said much less than I am reporting because he would begin a thought and then wave his hand and say "You know the rest of that." I showed him this text and he said it was a lot prettier than he actually talked but he wouldn't disagree with it. Part of why the kids like him by the way is that he listens a whole lot more than he talks.

"So, you're the man who teaches Driver Training."

"Well, that's my job title, yes."

"I'd like to know what you really do. The students say that you are one of the really fine people around school—a truly maximum dude."

"You really want to know?"

"I really want to know."

"I guess this sounds presumptuous but I think of myself as a Shaman—one who is involved in helping young men and women move through a rite of passage, and my job is getting them to think about this time in their lives. Most of them are almost sixteen and they know a lot more about life, and sex, and alcohol, and drugs, and money than their parents or their teachers give them credit for, and they are a lot more grown up and knowledgeable about the world than they get credit for, and they are physically pretty much what they're going to be. But we don't have any cultural rituals to acknowledge this. There's no ceremony, changing of clothes or roles or public statement that says "This isn't a kid anymore—this is a young adult." The only thing we do is give them a driver's license. But that's really important. Learning to drive a car means you move out of the back seat and into the driver's seat. You aren't a passenger anymore. Now you're in charge. You can go where you want to go. You have power now. So, that's what we talk about—that power."

"But what about actually learning to operate a vehicle?"

"Oh, that comes easily enough. Some driving time with suggestions, reading the manual—see they want all enough to work at it on their own. But I don't talk much about that. They have to pass a test and it usually takes care of itself."

"So, what do you talk about when you're out driving?"

"We talk about that power, opportunity, responsibility—about fears, about "someday" and "what if?" I listen a lot mostly. I'm not a parent. I'm not a schoolteacher, or a neighbor, or a shrink and they hardly ever see me except when it's just the two of us out in the car cruising around. So I'm safe to talk to. They tell me about love, and money, and plans—and they ask me what it was like when I was their age and what I wish I knew back then what I know now. Sometimes they ask me about the Navy and I tell them about the sea, and the wide world, and the stars at night. We even talk about God, life and death sometimes, but mostly I listen.

"I read somewhere about the Indians who had a special person whose job it was to explain to the young men about what's involved in being a brave member of the tribe, and I like to think that's kind of what I do. My job is to help the young into the tribe in a way that's good for the tribe as well as for them. I know it sounds corny, but it's what I do to make the world a better place."

"Would you take me out for a drive? My driving could be improved." And so we went, and so it was—my driving was improved along with my sense of place and purpose.

From Jack Perry, the kids learn both how to drive a car and drive a life, with care.

In closing this chapter, I am reminded of an older man who works as a crossing guard that I see each day. While he waits for the children to exit their building, he stands by the edge of the road, and with the biggest smile a human being can possibly muster, he joyfully gives every car that passes by two thumbs up and then points to you with his two index fingers as if to shout, "I hope YOU are having a fantastic day!"

Though I've never met this man, I would love to not only have this opportunity, but to have him in as a guest in my class to share his philosophy of life, because in his actions he has reaffirmed for me something that I have believed for a long time, and that is that it is not so much *what* you do in life, but rather *how* you do it that makes all the difference in the world. Here is a man who, it appears, has decided, "You know what? This is where my feet are planted in this universe, and I'm going to make the most of every breath I have to bring a little joy to people as they pass by." And let me tell you—he succeeds.

And, so, with all of the above examples in mind, I ask you to seriously ponder these questions and to articulate in writing your responses:

WHAT IS YOUR PHILOSOHY OF LIFE?

HOW DOES YOUR PHILOSOPHY OF LIFE RELATE TO YOUR TEACHING STYLE AND YOUR SENSE OF IDENTITY AS A TEACHER?

WHEN YOU WALK INTO YOUR CLASSROOM EACH DAY, WHAT IS THE "BIG PICTURE" OF WHAT YOU HOPE TO ACCOMPLISH WITH YOUR STUDENTS? WHAT IS IT THAT YOU SEE YOURSELF DOING?

"To live a single day and hear good teaching
is better than to live a hundred years
without knowing such teaching."
— Buddha

Chapter Four

The Most Important Day
of the School Year

I've been asked many times in my career if I would mind being observed by a colleague or a college student contemplating a career in teaching, and I always answer with the same response: "Yes, of course...and if it's possible I think it would be really beneficial if you could come on the first day of school, when I'm meeting the students for the first time."

"That sounds great," they usually say, "but may I ask why? Isn't that when you just hand out books?"

"To the contrary," I respond. "It is, in my opinion, the most important day of the school year, because it is on this day that you will either make or break some kind of rapport with your students, and that day will set the tone for the rest of the year."

What I thought I would do with this chapter is to ask you, my reader, if you suspend your present reality and pretend that you are a student in my high school class on the first day of school. Rather than telling you what I do on this day, I thought that it would be more useful for you to hear the actual words and see what I give my students as if you were them. Certainly what I say here is directly linked to my grade level and my curriculum, but I share it with the hope that if you find it useful, you would be able to adapt it to your style, identity, age group, and curriculum. And so the bell has rung and you have just taken your seat.

"Good morning, ladies and gentlemen. To those whom I have not had the pleasure of meeting before, my name is Mr. Perricone, but you can call me by my first name…Mr. (intentional silence as they try to figure out what I'm up to)…" I continue. "Oh, that was wicked funny," I say. (Laughter followed by a sigh of relief as they get that I was making a stupid joke I knew wasn't funny.) "Can anyone tell me what I just did? I violated the first rule of the first day of teaching, which is what? What do you think they teach us in college regarding the first day of school? You should never make any attempts at being what?" ("Funny!" someone retorts from the back of the room.) "And apparently I wasn't, so so far I'm right on track." (The snickers continue as they start to lighten up.)

"How am I supposed to be on the first day?"

"Mean and strict!" someone yells.

"That's right…so in the spirit of being mean would you please look at the first handout that I have placed on your desk.

AN INTRODUCTION TO HEALTH EDUCATION

1. MY EXPECTATIONS: What I expect of my students is never kept secret. This paper is intended to make you aware of my expectations so that our time together will be productive and serene from our first to our last day. Please keep this for future reference.

It is my opinion that education need not be boring. By the same token, I am not, nor should I be expected to be Jim Carrey. What is important is that you take responsibility for your own learning. Those who fail to see their role in the learning process can easily blame the system to support a stance of helplessness. I have learned to have little sympathy with those who maintain an apathetic attitude toward their learning while doing nothing but complain about their boring teachers and irrelevant classes. If you are dissatisfied with your education (and I was dissatisfied with much of mine), I hope that you will look not only at the faults of "the system" but at yourself as well to see how much you are willing to make it more vital. Are you just waiting for others to make your learning meaningful? How much are you willing to do to change those things you don't like? Are you accepting responsibility for putting something into the learning process?

(I stop at this point and say, "You know ladies and gentlemen, I like to think of what I do here each day as a dance—metaphorically speaking. Have you ever tried to dance with someone who is in a coma? It's not a lot of fun. So you could be really in the mood to dance one night but if your partner is just sitting there like a bump on a log, slouching in their chair, saying, 'This is really gay' (big laugh, though I deal with that issue later in the course), the dance is dead right there. So I ask you on this first day, again, metaphorically speaking, will you dance with me this semester? If you say 'yes' to me today we will have an incredible time together! I promise you. And I'll tell you right now that there are people who come to class every day with this attitude of 'I'm ready to dance, Mr. Perricone!' And there are others, and don't get me wrong—we all have bad days, who consistently come with their face on their hand looking almost barely alive—and you know what? I used to take responsibility for that person. I used to think, 'Hey, maybe I am so boring that it's unbearable for them.' But then I realized that there are people who go to a Barry Manilow concert and are bored. Can you imagine that?" (For those who don't recognize the name I say, "You know that guy who sings 'At the Copa, Copa Cabana.' That usually gains some recognition, and if not it just serves to make me feel old. "Ask your parents, they'll tell you who he is.")

"Anyway, do you want to know what one of my favorite quotes is? 'If you're bored, you're boring.' Have you ever noticed how many of the people who are constantly complaining about how bored they are, are some of the most boring people in the world? Monotony is a part of everyone's reality, and each of us is responsible for our own levels of boredom. If you are waiting for others to make your life interesting, I'm sorry, but you're going to have a long wait. By the same token, please be assured that I have had my share of really boring teachers. When I was in college I took a course entitled Introduction to Cinema, and I can't tell you how excited I was to take this class, knowing that I was going to learn the creative art of film making. Unfortunately for me, the semester that I took the course had the regular professor away on sabbatical, and we had a sub for him who turned out to be a real film maker from NYC so now I'm thinking, 'Hey, this is even better.' I could not have been more wrong.

"Picture if you will a very large man who has just rolled out of bed. He is unshaven, has a cigarette dangling from one side of his mouth, and his shirt is so far unbuttoned that we can see his navel. We are all feeling as though we are being held prisoner in this dingy room of a basement in the Fine Arts building for three and a half hours, three times a week listening to a man who spoke in an almost silent monotone voice while making no eye contact, saying inspiring things like 'And now we will turn to page 33 and read together.' I remembered thinking, 'If there is a hell—this is it. You have to listen to this man for eternity.' So, I'm very sensitive to this, and if you'll continue with my handout, I make the following promise to you:

I expect to give my very best to make this class interesting and stimulating, and therefore expect nothing less than your best efforts in return. Such effort includes excellent attendance, preparation for class, listening to and following directions, class participation, and completing assigned work on time. (Public affirmation.)

"If you are willing to give these few things, may I respectfully request that you raise your hand in front of your peers to make this class happen? If you are not, may I respectfully request that you drop the class and sign up for it again when you are ready to take it, because one person's negative energy can become a cancer to the group. Please feel free to talk to me after class if you feel you can't make that commitment." Semester after semester, every hand is up, because at this point they have come to see that I am their ally and that I want nothing more for them to learn and succeed.

I turn to a student and say, "Can you feel the vibes? This class is happening." (More laughter as the class is relaxing and realizing that I'm a real human being who really enjoys their company.) "Vibes is a 70s term for those of you who…never mind. OK, let's read on."

2. MATERIALS NEEDED EACH DAY: (Staying organized each day will really help you succeed)

    a. Assignment notebook
    b. Health notebook
    c. Assignment for the day (no excuses, please)
    d. Pen/pencile. Binder/folder for class handout
    f. Your mind and body ready to dance

"OK, now how many anarchists do we have in the room? Without trying to insult anyone's intelligence, can anyone tell me why all societies have laws? (The answer quickly comes "To maintain order" or "to protect our rights.") So none of you would want to live in a society where someone can just kill a member of your family and when you report it to the police they just say, 'Hey, that's what he's in to. Sorry.' So, good, the law exists to protect our rights. Let's keep reading."

3. WHAT ARE YOUR RIGHTS IN THIS CLASSROOM?
    TO LEARN: As a student it is your right and privilege to learn without distraction. No one has the right to violate another person's right to learn, and such violations will not be tolerated. Please show consideration to others.

"I know I didn't even have to say this because the vibes in this class are already so good. Can you feel the vibes? Sorry, I just had another 70s flashback."

4. WHAT ARE MY RIGHTS AS INTRUCTOR OF THIS COURSE?
    "This is very exciting for me. I have rights too! What are they?"
    TO TEACH: This is my job. I have earned my license to teach (I hold up my license at this point and explain to them that it took me six years to earn it and ten years of loans to pay for it), and therefore no one has the right to violate my right to do my job. (I would assume that if your parents were surgeons you would not step into the operating room in the middle of their work and yell, 'Hey, what's for supper?' Similarly, I respectfully request that my work not be interrupted.)

"For all the complaining that goes on about how much school stinks, I have found over the years that many enlightened people are interested in getting more than just a credit out of their classes, and it is out of respect for you that I will do everything that I can to uphold and protect your rights. Please remember at all times that this is your room and your class, and that the behavior and participation of each person will shape the type of learning that will occur. Because one person's behavior affects everyone else, I respectfully request that everyone in the class, and not just me, be responsible for classroom management.

"Have you ever noticed that if you throw a rock on a calm pond, it doesn't just sit there but it causes ripples that reverberate all the way across that pond? That's the way it is with us. We have energy that comes from us all day long that affects others for better or for worse. One person's behavior can become a cancer to an entire class. I'm going to pretend that I'm a student in this class right now. (I move to an empty desk at the back of the room and sit down.) Now suppose this person in front of me is being obnoxious and annoying and distracting everyone in the class. Do you know what people do? They look at me as if to say, 'Deal with it, Mr. Perricone—this is your class.' I'm suggesting to you today, ladies and gentlemen, that no, this is not my class—it is our class. So, all I'm asking you is that if you are sitting next to such a person that you kindly lean into them and say, "Excuse me, but you're violating my right to learn." (This usually gets a good laugh, but my students have totally gotten the point I'm making.)

The handout continues on the back:

THE LAW: TO BE FOLLOWED WITHOUT EXCEPTION

1. Be on time, prepared, and ready to work from the beginning to the end of class. (Please let me dismiss the class.) "I start from the second the bell rings, and to give your parents more for their tax dollar I teach until it rings again. I realize that you have other classes to get to, so I promise I will try to never go more than 15 seconds after the bell, but please don't start packing up until I'm done, OK? Thank you."

2. Please raise your hand when you wish to speak and wait to be called upon. "This is not because I'm neurotic about order or because

I had needs for power that went unfulfilled from my childhood and now I'm getting even, but what raising your hand means is that you are now on microphone—just like if you were on the *Oprah* show. You can now be heard, and I can take your idea and toss it to someone else in the class—and this so adds to making for the best possible learning environment. All right? Great."

3. Please listen to others with all your heart and soul. I will do the same.

"If you want to really know what your teachers are looking for on the first day of school, it's what I call 'listening eyes'—eyes that are focused and just thirsting for more. Eyes that are saying, "Tell us some more stories about Barry Manilow, Grandpa." (More snickers, as they continue to loosen up with me and grow more comfortable.)

4. Please treat others as you would like to be treated.

"This seems like such a simple rule of human interaction that you would think we all would have picked up in kindergarten, but I'm sure as you walk the halls each day, you've discovered that many missed this simple lesson along the way. I'm going to make an appeal to your sense of dignity from this first day and simply ask you to always extend respect to each other in your language and your actions—just basic human respect. Each day I will have a different quote on the board and today's says:

> *"Manners are like the zero in arithmetic;*
> *they may not be much in themselves,*
> *but they are capable of adding a great deal*
> *to the value of everything else."*
> *– Freya Stark*

"Let me ask you a question. Have you ever been in an arena where everyone is handed an unlit candle when they walk in? And then one is lit, and then another, and in about an hour the entire arena is illuminated by every person's lit candle. This may sound a little corny, but I like to think of manners as just that—good energy spreading among people. What a difference it can make in the quality of our lives.

From our first day together I'll tell you right up front that I love being a teacher and very much enjoy relating to people on a *mutual respect* level. It has been my experience that human interaction can be tremendously rewarding when such respect exists. I will always extend this consideration to you, and ask only that you return this in kind. Thank you. (Today is clean slate day.)

"If you're wondering what 'clean slate day' means, it simply means this. If I have ever had any kind of negative interaction with anyone in this room—one of the advantages of my growing older is that I have forgotten. As far as I know right now, you are a dignified human being deserving of my respect, and I am going to move forward from this moment with that assumption." (I cannot begin to tell you the sense of relief that this brings to some students' eyes who feel as though they have been judged and stereotyped for so long that they don't have a prayer to start fresh with anyone. It's a huge statement that goes a long way)

The rest of my handout deals with the "business" or "logistical" aspects of my class such as my use of objectives, assignments, absences, and my grading system. I've included the entire handout in the appendix of this book for those who might find it useful, but shared what I did above because I am so often asked, "John, what is your approach to discipline problems?" My answer has always been that I can count on less than one hand the number of disciplinary referrals I have written in twenty-two years, and I attribute this to this first day handout and its accompanying discussion that is one hundred percent "preventative" by its nature rather than being "reactive" and "punitive." From the first day, I make it very clear to my students that I love my work with them, that I am on their side, and that I have created these expectations to better serve them—and they get it, year after year. Interestingly, if I've ever had a behavioral issue with a student, almost without exception, it is someone who missed this first day discussion and its accompanying "bonding." Indeed, I often find the students correcting each other's behavior with statements like, "Shhh…. He's talking." When I witness this, I feel as though I've died and gone to teacher Heaven (where all administrators support you and the copy machine never breaks).

Now I realize at this point you may be thinking, "John, you've asked us to reflect upon our philosophical identities and how that affects our teaching. How do you communicate your philosophy to your students?" Again, I believe there is nothing more important to do on the first day of school than share this deepest part of ourselves with our students. Immediately after covering my first day handout, I say the following to my students (and again, if you agree with me, this would obviously be modified and adapted to your age group and subject matter):

"Ladies and gentlemen, if you would just sit back and relax now, I'd like to share some personal philosophy with you. On the eve of my very first student teaching assignment some twenty-three years ago, I was sitting in my apartment, thinking, "What the heck am I going to say to my students tomorrow on the first day of school, because it seemed to me that this was the most important day of the year—the day that I would either make or break some kind of rapport with my students. And what I came to that night is a question that I've been throwing out to my students on the first day of school ever since, and that is the question of 'Why?'

"Why are you doing this? Why are you getting an education? And I don't want you to give me the answer you think that I want to hear unless it's what you truly feel. I want you to know from our first day that you have the right in this class to speak openly and honestly about your feelings. I also want you to know that I wasn't happy with my own answer to that question until about my junior year of college, and prior to that I had felt that the educational system was simply something that had imposed itself on my life and that it was just one more huge wall I had to climb over before I could get to what I wanted from life.

"May I ask how many of you in this room are over sixteen years of age? (Some hands go up.) Look at these people. Legally, they don't have to be here. (I approach one of these students.) May I ask why you are here? Why are you getting an education?"

"So I can get a good job some day."

"And why would you want a good job?" I ask.

"So I can make money" is a very typical response.

"Stay with me now. And why do you want to make money?"

"So I can live—like, duh."

"And this is where we always end up in this questioning, ladies and gentlemen, and it's at this point that I will ask all of you this question, and you don't have to answer it out loud—and that question is "What do you live for? What do you personally live for?" (Silence in the room.)

"What do I live for?" someone eventually says. "I guess I live for what everyone else is living for... I guess I just want to be happy."

"Exactly! Isn't that the universal human quest? I mean I'm 45 years old and in my entire life I have never met anyone who has said, 'You know what? There's a lot of things I want in life but I'll tell you what I definitely don't want: I don't want to be happy and I definitely don't want to be fulfilled! Just keep that crap away from me!' Ladies and gentlemen, I've never met this person. So if it's true that the pursuit of happiness is the universal human quest, the next question has to be, 'How does one attain that, especially since what makes one person happy in this class may be very different from what makes another feel the same?'

"Let me share with you, if I may now, a reading from page twenty-two of a book written by Harold Kushner entitled *When All You've Ever Really Wanted Isn't Enough*. Imagine someone gave you a billion dollars today and for two years you did it all—you traveled across the world, went skydiving and bungie jumping, went to every amusement park on the planet and on and on and on and at the end of all of that you discovered that you really weren't all that happy. There was still a deep hole within you. That's what this book is about. Well, on page twenty-two, Harold Kushner makes this statement, and whenever I read something to you in this class, I'm never asking you to agree with it. All I ask is that you think about it, and turn it around in your head. He says this:

> **America's Declaration of Independence guarantees every one of us the right to the pursuit of happiness. But because the Declaration is a political document and not a religious one, it does not warn us of the frustrations of trying to exercise that right, because the pursuit of happiness is the wrong goal. You don't become happy by pursuing happiness. You become happy by living a life that means something.**

"For the sake of discussion, let's assume that Kushner is on to something here—that happiness is not an end in itself but rather a by-product of living a meaningful life. It would seem then that the next question we have to ask is: 'How does one live a meaningful life?'

"I am 45 years old now, and I have had some time to observe others and myself in pursuit of this thing we call happiness, and if you'll indulge me for a moment, I 'd like to speak to three paths I've seen many people take in pursuit of this universal yet elusive goal. One path I've seen many people take is the path of IGNORANCE. 'I know nothing, so nothing bothers me!' Why do you always have to be talking about nuclear disarmament and children dying in third-world nations? C'mon, there's a sale at the mall!' Now we could talk for hours about whether or not ignorance is bliss, and perhaps the way to go through life, but I saw a bumper sticker recently that put a different spin on this and it simply said, 'If you think education is expensive, try ignorance.'

"Another path I've seen many people take in their lives, some of which were able to come back and talk about it, and others who didn't survive to do that is the path of some form of DRUG-INDUCED EUPHORIA. 'Man, I've got this drug coursing through my veins now, and I'm really high.' My experience has been that most people (if they don't die in the process) eventually realize that at best, this was an attempt to meet some unfulfilled needs in their lives and that it never really amounted to any lasting fulfillment. Some may have to really hit bottom before they realize it, and that many may need help of the medical kind to recover, but the result is always the same—no happiness at the end of this tunnel.

"The highest path that I believe any of us can take in the pursuit of meaning and fulfillment, ladies and gentlemen—and again I'm not asking you to agree with me but just to hear it as another offering as you sort through and create your own philosophy of life, is the path of SELF-UNDERSTANDING—the path of truly knowing yourself.

"You see, we are all born at some point A, and then we live our lives and do what at point B?"

"We die," someone sullenly responds.

"That's right. And to the best of our knowledge, we are the only living creatures on the face of this earth who can consciously enhance the quality of our lives, or conversely, we can destroy ourselves. We embody this amazing power of our 'will,' which allows us to shape our destiny. I can take a step forward, or I can move my foot back. I can go to college or not. I can choose to treat people with dignity and respect or I can assume that every person I encounter is a back-stabbing scum. I can take this pen in my hand—an inanimate object—and I can write beautiful poetry with it, or (pointing it at a student) I can take his eye out with it. Do you see what I'm trying to say? This is our unique gift as human beings. You tap into the power of your own will, and you'll be overdosing. I'm overdosing right now just talking about it. Somebody call 911!

"Now back to the path of self-understanding. It seems to me that the better you know yourself—your strengths and weaknesses, your likes and dislikes, what you want from life and what you don't want etc.—the better you can live that life between point A and point B that is going to be the most fulfilling, and thereby the most meaningful and happy. I was so close to becoming a lawyer because it was something my mother wanted for me, but as I came to better know myself—and it took a lot of work, my life's path became much clearer—and here I am before you, doing my best to embody you with the tools to know yourself and find your life's meaning. That's what this entire course is about—knowing yourself mentally, physically, socially, emotionally, and some would even say spiritually—or at least philosophically.

"I'd like to close our first class together by sharing a brief letter that a principal wrote to his teachers on the first day of school, and I share this with you because it lays the foundation to my whole approach to teaching.

"Here's what the principal said:

Dear Teacher,

I am a survivor of a concentration camp. My eyes saw what no man should witness:

Gas chambers built by learned engineers. Children poisoned by educated physicians. Infants killed by trained nurses. Women and babies shot and burned by high school and college graduates.

So, I am suspicious of education.

My request is this: Help your children become human. Your efforts must never produce learned monsters, skilled psychopaths, or educated Eichmanns. Reading, writing, and arithmetic are important, only if they serve to make our children more humane.

"And so more than having just a bunch of facts every day—which are important so that we can have an intelligent discussion—I hope that this principal's letter serves to demonstrate that facts alone are not enough. Some incredibly bright people throughout history have committed horrific atrocities. More than having just a bunch of facts, it is my hope that you leave here each day with a deeper sense of who you are, and perhaps a deeper appreciation of the experience of your humanity. If we accomplish that together this semester, I hope you'll agree that we have accomplished something worthwhile. There's the bell. Thank you for coming and I'll look forward to seeing you tomorrow."

"ONE MAN GETS NOTHING BUT DISCORD OUT OF A PIANO;
ANOTHER GETS HARMONY. NO ONE CLAIMS THAT THE PIANO
IS AT FAULT. LIFE IS ABOUT THE SAME. THE DISCORD IS THERE,
AND THE HARMONY IS THERE. PLAY IT CORRECTLY
AND IT WILL GIVE FORTH THE BEAUTY;
PLAY IT FALSELY, AND IT WILL GIVE FORTH UGLINESS.
LIFE IS NOT AT FAULT."
– NINON DE L'ENCLOS

CHAPTER FIVE

WHAT'S IN IT FOR ME?

What makes us tick? Why do we behave the way we do? Is human behavior driven by impulse and appetite? Why does competition bring out the best in some individuals and teams who get "psyched up" and the worst in others who get "psyched out"? Why are some people ready to sacrifice their lives for what they believe in, while others are so apathetic they seem to care about nothing? Are we basically violent beings, or are we primarily peaceful loving beings? Is the pursuit of pleasure our basic drive, or do we need to seek a higher meaning in life? Serious students of human nature have put forth all of these theories.

Perhaps in understanding some of the various psychological theories of personality, we can better understand our own and our students' thinking and actions. Perhaps to some degree we can direct our own destinies, and better enable our students to direct theirs.

Just about everyone who has offered suggestions about what motivates us has theorized that human being have both *needs* and *drives* that direct behavior. A drive may push us to seek pleasure, to feel powerful, to love, or to find meaning in life. Regardless of what it is we may be seeking, it seems that *everything we do is motivated by some kind of search for a reward or a fear of punishment*. (When I ask my students on the first day of school why they are getting an education, some say, "To get a good job so that I can live a better life." Clearly this is the reward. Others have said, "If I don't come to school, my parents will kick my butt!" Here again, an obvious case of avoiding punishment.) I have challenged my students for twenty-two years to come up with an exception, hoping that maybe some day someone will, but to date, no one has accomplished this end. Some have in past years raised the issue of the Kamikaze pilots, or, in more recent times, the suicide bombers. Almost as quickly as they raise the question you can see the light coming on in their eyes to the realization that in the context of these peoples' customs and beliefs, clearly they were and are seeking what they believe are rewards—whether those rewards are honor or the promise of Heavenly paradise.

So if one can accept the basic psychological premise that all behaviors (from scratching our heads, to driving our cars, to serving on the PTA, to acting obnoxiously in a classroom, to becoming a teacher, etc.) are an attempt to satisfy a human need or needs, then we can begin to embrace a deeper understanding of what being a teacher does or does not mean to us (whether or not it satisfies our needs), and whether or not our teaching has meaning and value to our students' lives (does it help them to satisfy their needs?)

I remember quite vividly being twelve years old and sitting with my father and his friend Walter Thompson at Lil Leon's ice cream store in Vestal, N.Y., and I remember on that particular day that I was lamenting the fact that I had no idea what I wanted to do for a career when I grew up. Mr. Thompson responded, "You know what, John? There are a lot of people in their fifties who have no idea what they want to do." I recall thinking, "Well, that wasn't very helpful." But then he went on to utter a sentence that changed the path of my life. He said, "You know what, John, I go to a job every day at IBM that I can't stand so that I can make enough money to do the things that I want to do." I'm not sure what vocabulary skills I was in possession of at that time, but I responded with something along the lines of "Well, if that works for you, Mr. Thompson, I'm happy for you."

I remember going home and chewing on what he had said for some time, and I remember thinking, "Man, nine to five is a huge chunk of your life to hate what you do every day just so you can go on vacation for two weeks and spend those two weeks thinking about how much you hate the thought of going back to your job." For whatever it's worth to my reader, I've attended over 250 funerals in my life, and not even once in hearing someone's life recalled have I heard someone say, "Here lies Joe. He drove a Porsche, had a huge swimming pool in his backyard, and one of the biggest boats you've ever seen." In the final analysis, and when our lives are being recollected, these things don't seem to be what anyone remembers or even care to remember about us, and yet from the moment we are born the culture we live in teaches us to measure success by what we make and how much we've accumulated, and consciously or not, we often cannot but help to use this script as a backdrop for evaluating our sense of "worth" in this life. It's a tough mindset to overcome, and each of us who chooses service over material rewards have to come to terms with the dissonance that our culture may create for us at every turn in this regard. One of my favorite stories on this very subject is called "The Fisherman" and it goes like this:

> The American investment banker was at the pier of a small coastal Mexican village when a small boat with just one fisherman docked. Inside the small boat were several large yellow-finned tuna. The American complimented the Mexican on the quality of his fish and asked him how long it took to catch them.
>
> The Mexican replied, "Only a little while."
>
> The American than asked why he didn't stay out longer and catch more fish.

The Mexican said he had enough to support his family's immediate needs.

The American then asked, "But what do you do with the rest of your time?"

The Mexican fisherman said, "I'll sleep late, fish a little, play with my children, take siesta with my wife Maria, stroll into the village each evening where I sip wine and play guitar with my amigos. I have a full and busy life."

The American scoffed, "I am a Harvard MBA and could help you. You should spend more time fishing and, with the proceeds, buy a bigger boat and with the proceeds of a bigger boat you could buy several boats. Eventually you would have a fleet of fishing boats. Instead of selling to a middleman you would sell directly to the processor, eventually opening your own cannery. You would control the product, processing, and distribution. You would need to leave this small coastal fishing village and move to Mexico City, then L.A. and eventually New York City where you will run your expanding enterprise."

The Mexican fisherman asked, "But how long will this all take?"

To which the American replied, "Fifteen to twenty years."

"But what then?"

The American laughed and said, "That's the best part. When the time is right you would announce an IPO and sell your company stock to the public and become very rich—you would make millions."

"Millions...then what?"

The American said, "Then you would retire, move to a small coastal fishing village where you would sleep late, fish a little, play with your kids, take siesta with your wife, stroll to the village in the evenings where you could sip wine and play guitar with your amigos."

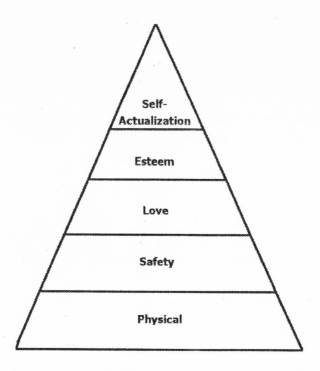

Psychologist Abraham Maslow states in his theory of human behavior that all human beings have the same needs (physical, safety, love, esteem, and self-actualization) and that these needs are hierarchical in nature. By this he simply meant, as diagramed above, that we cannot satisfy our higher level needs until our lower level needs are met. Our most basic needs are physical (food, water, oxygen). If you've been fortunate enough in life to know where your next meal is coming from, Maslow says that you can climb to the next level of need fulfillment—that of safety, which includes both physical and emotional security. The next need up the ladder is love, which most of us fulfill through our families, friends, and pets. (Maslow argued that there were probably more people suffering in our mental institutions because this one need had gone unmet in life than for any other reason). He said if you have been so fortunate to have had these needs met, the next need is for that of esteem, or a feeling of self-worth and self-respect. And lastly, if you have been so blessed to have had all these needs met, he said you could then climb to what he considered to be the highest level of human functioning—that of self-actualization. He referred to this process as "becoming fully human" or "developing one's full potential." In looking at self-actualized people, Maslow said, we see that people are involved in interests outside of themselves. They are devoted to something that is very precious to them and that is bigger than they are. One pursues justice, another wisdom, another truth—each is truly happy pursuing a human value that transcends an individual life. Maslow cited people like Mother Theresa and Martin Luther King as examples of "self-actualized" individuals.

If I asked you to superimpose Maslow's theory of need fulfillment over your career, how many of these needs would you say are fulfilled by teaching?

I know that in my own career, teaching has filled all of these needs and then some. My cup runneth over. It's difficult for me to imagine a vocation where one has the opportunity to give so much and to receive so much in return.

"REAL TEACHING IS PATIENCE AND COURAGE
AND ENDURANCE AND PERCEPTION.
IT DROWNS THE TEACHER.
BUT THEN, SO DOES ANYTHING DONE WELL."
– PAM BROWN

CHAPTER SIX

WHAT WAS I SUPPOSED TO BE TEACHING?

Early in my career I had the pleasure and the honor of attending an education seminar that was facilitated by famed anthropologist Dr. Ashley Montagu. He reminded all of us who were present that that the Latin root of the word "education" was "educare," which means to love, nurture, and to help grow. He also told us that sadly he didn't see much of this going on in our schools, but rather what he observed was a lot of "instruction."

My personal feeling is that good teaching must incorporate both love and nurturance combined with meaningful instruction, because if we only love and nurture minus an instructional curriculum, what do we produce? Stupid kids who feel really good about themselves.

If we only instruct in the absence of love and nurturing, we end up with a teacher writing a poem of regret as Naomi White did when she wrote the following in 1943:

I Taught Them All

I have taught in high school for ten years. During that time I have given assignments, among others, to a murderer, a pugilist, a thief and an imbecile. The murderer was a quiet little boy who sat on the front seat and regarded me with pale blue eyes; the pugilist lounged by the window and let loose at intervals in a raucous laugh that startled even the geraniums; the thief was a gay-hearted Lothario with a song on his lips; and the imbecile, a shifty eyed little animal seeking the shadows.

The murderer awaits death in the state penitentiary; the pugilist lost an eye in a brawl in Hong Kong; the thief, by standing on tip-toe, can see the window of my room from the county jail; and the once gentle-eyed little moron beats his head against a padded wall in an asylum.

All these pupils once sat in my room, sat and looked at me across worn brown desks. I must have been a great help to these pupils…I taught them the rhyming scheme of the Elizabethan sonnet and how to diagram a complex sentence.

One of the most powerful experiences that shaped me as a teacher earlier in my career was reading and then seeing the movie adaptation of Bel Kaufman's *Up the Down Staircase*. In one of its more powerful and gripping scenes, an eighteen-year-old high school student finds herself falling in love with her English teacher, and, knowing that her feelings for him can never come to fruition, she begins to contemplate suicide. Feeling that she has nothing to lose, she decides in a final act of desperation to pour her feelings out to him in an essay. Shaken and overwhelmed with trepidation, she slowly approaches his desk and hands the essay to him, after which she returns to her seat. Less than five minutes later, he calls her to his desk, and with his red pen in hand, begins to correct her grammar in the margins, never once acknowledging the content of her writing. Later that night, this young woman takes her life.

So, it appears that, as teachers, much of what we are teaching between the lines transcends the curriculum we have mastered. As I mentioned earlier, the teacher I admired and revisited most often taught the curriculum that I most despised. As one retired colleague recently told me, "You know John, the first twenty-five years of my career I taught math—the last five years I taught people. What a difference it made in my life and the lives of my students."

After twenty-two years in the classroom, I am convinced more than ever that the ultimate purpose of our work (outside of giving our students the skills to help them make it in the "real world") is one of helping them discover their talents and hopefully a deeper appreciation of their humanity and their unique place in the universe.

> "WHAT WE DO FOR OURSELVES DIES WITH US.
> WHAT WE DO FOR OTHERS AND THE WORLD IS,
> AND REMAINS...IMMORTAL."
> – ALBERT PINE

CHAPTER SEVEN

ZEN AND THE ART OF TEACHING: AVOIDING BURNOUT

I have been deeply honored over the years to speak to groups of would-be teachers excited and ready to take on the world. Their energy and excitement is invigorating and renewing for me. As I field their questions about life in the classroom, inevitably someone will ask me, "What advice do you think will most help us in our careers as teachers?"

To this question, I say these two things: "Try very hard in your career not to confuse FEAR with RESPECT. Though the outside results may look the same, below the surface, they are worlds apart. It deeply saddens me when I see young teachers enter their careers with this look of intimidation in their eyes that says—*you'd better not mess with me, or else.* They are doing this, I believe, because sadly, this behavior pattern was probably modeled for them as they were growing up, and also because I believe that they are afraid that if they don't manifest this look, they might lose control, and then all hell would break loose. Nothing in my experience could be further from the truth. You cannot demand respect from your students, but you can command it through your actions—especially by demonstrating respect for them. And if you earn the respect of your students, you cannot imagine the joy that awaits you in your profession."

And then I tell them, "You know, people often ask me: 'John, in your thirty-two years of training with Master Ochiai (a man who I have already credited with being the sole impetus for my choosing teaching as my vocation), what would you say is the most valuable piece of wisdom that you have learned from him that you can impart to us?'

"Well," I say, "there is much to condense when you've had thirty-two years to bask in the wisdom of a man who spent sixteen years of his life in a Zen monastery and who has unselfishly dedicated his life's energy to helping others realize their potential, but since you've asked the question, I will answer in a word, and that word is "shoshin."

"Shoshin translates 'cherish your beginner's mind.' Remember how exciting a new venture is at its very beginning, but with time that excitement is slowly extinguished? Would you all agree that anything we do in this life with repetition has the potential to become monotonous, whether it be our jobs, our relationships, or even a hobby?" They all shake their heads in agreement. "Mr. Ochiai began his training in the martial arts when he was six years old, and at sixty-five now, he still teaches with all the freshness, excitement, and exhilaration that I see residing in your eyes, and do you know why that is, or how that is possible? Because of shoshin. Each day when he enters the floor to teach class he tells himself, 'This is the first day that I have ever taught, and it may be my last. I will teach this class with every ounce of my being as if this is the first time that I have ever seen these students, and with the realization that it may be the last chance that I will ever have to teach them again.'

"I can state unequivocally that he has lived and breathed this philosophy each and every day that I have experienced him teach over the past thirty-two years. It has been a powerful reinforcer that a person's philosophy of life and teaching can be so much more than words spoken, but literally the foundation to a life lived, and lived so well."

I cannot begin to tell you how many times this philosophy has served me in my career. Because I teach the Health curriculum, I do, unlike many other teachers, literally repeat my lesson five times a day. By the last period of the day, as I'm walking down the hall to my class hallucinating about my pillow on my bed at home, I say to myself, "shoshin," and with that consciousness of what my teacher has demonstrated for me, I give everything that I have to share the same energy with the last class of the day that I gave my first.

As an interesting aside, a beautiful and profound metaphor is born out of Master Ochiai's years of training. When someone begins their karate training, they enter the floor with a white belt on—the beginner's rank. Quite interestingly, after 59 years of training, Mr. Ochiai's blackbelt has returned to a shade of white—a perfect symbol of enlightenment. After years and years of training, both his heart and his belt have returned to the beginner's state of being—new, fresh, excited, and passionate to go.

Master Ochiai at sixty-five

> "THE MEDIOCRE TEACHER TELLS.
> THE GOOD TEACHER EXPLAINS.
> THE SUPERIOR TEACHER DEMONSTRATES.
> THE GREAT TEACHER INSPIRES."
> – WILLIAM ARTHUR WARD

CHAPTER EIGHT

CHILDREN PUNISHED BY REWARDS

In this chapter I get to blow off some steam that has been brewing inside me for as long as I have been teaching. The following is a "Guest Viewpoint" article that I wrote for our local *Press & Sun-Bulletin* in Binghamton, N.Y. I am not exaggerating when I say that as soon as it went to print the phone rang off the hook for two weeks with comments from parents, teachers, and administrators who all in effect were saying, "Thank you for saying this. It's needed saying for a long time." Many teachers told me that they hung the article over their office desks as a reminder of its content. So let's take a quick stroll down Psych. 101 lane:

> "Hey guys, would you mind giving me a hand moving some of these desks to another room?"

"Sure, Mr. Perricone—what's in it for us?"

"What do you mean?" I ask, somewhat dejected.

"You know, maybe some extra credit, or a few points on your average?"

I stare at them in disbelief—they sense my discomfort, and the issue is dropped as they scurry to help me with the desks.

As both a high school educator who loves teaching and as a parent, I have grave concerns about a mindset that I have witnessed evolve over the past twenty years in many of our young people—a mindset that I believe my own profession, and many parents are unwittingly, yet largely responsible for. Specifically, my concern relates to an emphasis in our elementary and middle schools on the use of external rewards or "perks" (pizza parties, candy, etc.) that are used in an attempt to motivate (or bribe) our students and children to read, study, perform, or behave. Though well intentioned, study after study clearly suggest that these practices are counterproductive because a child promised a treat for learning or acting responsibly has been given every reason to stop doing so when there is no longer a reward to be gained. Simultaneously, intrinsic motivation (an interest in doing something for its own sake) quickly erodes and is soon lost to extrinsic motivation (completion of an activity or task is seen chiefly as a prerequisite for obtaining something else). Kohn (1993) argues that the reason this happens is that when someone says "Do *this* and you will get that," it automatically devalues "*this*." The recipient of the reward figures that if they have to be bribed, it must be something they wouldn't want to do for its own sake. How much sadder a message could we communicate to our kids if our goal is one of inspiring lifelong learning for its inherent worth? Is it naive, living in a culture that celebrates and glorifies external incentives, to think that our message to our children and students should be that the reward for reading a great book is a story that inspired and moved them, and not coupons to Pizza Hut? And that the reward for helping someone in need is the knowledge that one has eased another's burden?

At least two dozen studies have shown that people expecting to receive a reward for completing a task (or for doing it successfully) simply do not perform as well as those who expect nothing (Kohn, 1993). The most compelling explanation for this finding is that *rewards cause people to lose interest in whatever they were rewarded for doing*, and this is especially true in the mistaken practice of externally rewarding a child to do something that he or she already found to be internally satisfying (playing the piano, participating in a sport etc.). In one representative study, young children were introduced to an unfamiliar beverage called Kefir. Some were just asked to drink; others were praised lavishly for doing so; a third group was promised treats if they drank enough. Those children who received either verbal or tangible rewards consumed more of the beverage than other children, as one might predict. But a week later, these children found it significantly less appealing as they did before, whereas children who were offered no rewards liked it just as much as, if not more than, they had earlier (Birch, 1984). If we substitute reading, or doing math, or acting generously for drinking Kefir, we begin to glimpse the destructive nature of extrinsic reward systems. In another study, Lepper (1973) and his colleagues gave 51 pre-schoolers a chance to draw with magic markers—something most children find appealing. Some were told that if they drew pictures, they would each receive a certificate decorated with a red ribbon and gold star. Between a week and two weeks later, the children were observed in their classrooms. Those who had been told they would receive a certificate now seemed less interested in drawing with magic markers than those not promised a reward—and less interested than they themselves had been before the reward was offered. The experiments came to the same conclusion that extrinsic reward reduces intrinsic motivation. The data suggests that the more we want children to *want* to do something, the more counterproductive it will be to reward them for doing it. Four other studies, each conducted by a different experimenter and published in different journals, concluded the following:

1. Rewards can have one effect on quantity and another on quality.

2. Professional artists do less creative work when the work is commissioned in advance for a reward.

3. Those extrinsically motivated use less sophisticated learning strategies in completing a task.

4. Rewards are least effective (counter productive) when people get these rewards for doing things that are optimally challenging.

5. People offered rewards tend to choose easier tasks, are more illogical in problem solving strategies and less creative than non-rewarded subjects working on the same problems.

Kohn (1993) agrees that rewards work or their use would not be so widely practiced. The reason they work is that they are so easy to apply. "It takes talent and time to help people develop character, self-control, and the commitment to behave responsibly—it takes no patience, talent, or effort to announce "keep quiet and here's what you will get," he states.

The implications of these studies and the evidence of our own experiences should give us pause. If the question is, "Do rewards motivate students?" the answer is, "Absolutely! They motivate students to get rewards." Unfortunately, such motivation is often bought at the expense of interest in, a lack of connection to, and excellence at whatever our children and students are doing. Because the potential payoff—one of our children valuing learning for the sake of learning—is priceless, it seems nothing less than crucial for parents, teachers, and school leaders to rethink what has become an assumed and common practice.

"At all times I must be aware of the possibility of no tomorrow, and the possibility of many different tomorrows. Without an adequate comprehension of both possibilities, my vision of today is impaired."
— Joseph Martin

Chapter Nine

Making Our Mortality Our Ally

Toward the end of my course, I close my semester by engaging my students in a discussion about aging, the life cycle, loss, death, and developing their ever-evolving philosophies of life. I forewarn them that although this may sound like a really depressing way to bring closure to our time together, my intentions could not be further from this end. I reassure them that far from being morbid, it is my goal through these discussions to illuminate and accentuate their experience of their lives.

At some point in this dialogue I raise this question: "If you knew that you only had two days left to live, how would you want to spend them?"

A variety of responses spew forward ranging from, "I'd get the hell out of school—that's for sure!" to "I'd want to spend that time with friends and family."

I ask them again, "If you really knew this—not just intellectually, but right down to your bone marrow that you only had two days left in this world, do you think that your perception of life during those two days would be different?"

They all agree it would be.

"How would life be different?" I ask. "Would you be more or less likely to engage in petty arguments with friends and family?"

"Less," they say.

"Would you be more or less aware of the birds chirping in the trees on your walk home?"

"More," they concede.

I'll never forget one girl, upon my raising this question, raising her hand and saying, "You know what, Mr. Perricone, as corny as this may sound, I believe that if I were really in that state, I would actually perceive the air in this room touching my face. I'd probably even notice the doorknob on the way out of class."

"So," I say, "it has been the consensus of my students for the 22 years that I've been teaching that if they truly knew that death was imminent, suddenly life would burst into vivid interest—that relationships to others would become more cherished and more authentic, and that life in general would be deeply enriched." (I demonstrate this visually by taking a small piece of white paper [life] and holding a larger sheet of black paper [death] behind it. They clearly see that the black paper does not dilute the white paper, but rather enhances and illuminates it.)

"If what you're saying is true, what's keeping any of us right now from living our lives at this level of awareness, authenticity, and appreciation?" They quickly see that the answer to this question lies in the assumption that we "have forever." It is at this point that I introduce them to my final, and frankly speaking, my favorite assignment of the year, which I have entitled "The Lifeline." The assignment in its entirety follows below, and I hope, as I am approaching closure to this book, that you will take the time to complete this experience. I've had many students tell me that taking this journey has literally changed their lives.

SOME PHILOSOPHY

Each of us makes countless decisions that affect our lives and the lives of those around us to some degree. Many of the decisions are of very little importance, such as whether or not to go to the movies, where to have dinner, or what to wear. A few decisions are truly momentous—whom to marry (or to marry at all), what career to pursue; and for some of us caught up in a war or facing personal tragedy, our decisions may literally determine life or death. Socrates (469 B.C.) believed in his own time (and I think he would still believe if he were alive today) that these decisions that we base our lives upon must be questioned, examined, and criticized if we are to live truly good and fulfilling lives. His teaching was simply that "the unexamined life is not worth living." This is not a truth of physics or of mathematics that one can prove with deductions from axioms or experiments, but an appeal to our sense of dignity as rational creatures.

Most of us, many philosophers would argue, make even the most important decisions without really asking ourselves what principles we are basing our choices on, and whether those principles are truly worthy of our respect. When war comes, for example, many go off to fight and die with hardly more than a passing thought about whether it is ever morally right to kill another person. A student spends ten years of his life studying to become a doctor simply because Mom and Dad always wanted it. A man and woman drift into a marriage, have children, buy a house and settle down, and only twenty years later does one of them ask, "What am I doing here?" Socrates had a theory about how each of us ought to examine our lives, subjecting it to critical analysis and questioning. The theory rested on these principles:

1. The unexamined life is not worth living. To be truly human, and thereby truly happy, each man and woman must subject one's life and convictions to critical testing.

2. There are objectively valid principles of thought and action, which must be followed if we are to live good lives—lives both happy and just. It isn't true, Socrates argued, that every person's way of life is just as good as every other's. Some people are unjust, self-indulgent, obsessed with worthless goals, estranged from their fellow man, confused and blind about what is truly important, and they are incapable of either living or dying with grace and dignity. Such people, Socrates said, need to find the truth and then live in accordance with it.

3. This leads us to the question: Where does one find the truth? The truth, according to Socrates, lies within each of us—not in the stars, or in tradition, or in religious books, or in the opinions of the masses. Each of us, he argued, has within us, however hidden, the true principles of right thinking and acting. In the end, therefore, no one can teach anyone else the truth about life, and it is only through relentless, critical self-examination that one may reveal it.

In the spirit of such examination, please complete the following assignment. This experience, though potentially thought provoking, is not meant to be morbid; rather it is a tool that you can use in exploring the meaning of death and hopefully for the purpose of creating a more conscious and meaningful life.

DEATH AND THE MEANING OF LIFE

I accept the existentialist view that the acceptance of death is vitally related to the discovery of meaning and purpose in life. One of our distinguishing characteristics as human beings is our ability to grasp the concept of the future and thus the inevitability of death. Our ability to do so gives meaning to our existence, for it makes every act and every moment count. In his book *Is There an Answer to Death?* Koestenbaum (1976) develops the idea that our awareness of death compels us to see our lives in totality and to seek real and ultimate answers. As Koestenbaum writes: "Many people think of death as unreal, as just beyond the horizon, as something they should postpone thinking about—in fact, as an event that shouldn't even be mentioned. As a result, they are incapable of experiencing their lives as a whole—of forming any total life plan."

The meaning of our lives, then, depends on the fact that we are finite beings. By honestly accepting our mortality, we enable ourselves to define the quality of life we want. What we do with our lives counts (or at least it can count). We can choose to become all that we are capable of becoming and strive to live our lives at the highest expression of our humanity, or we can passively let life slip by us. We can settle for letting events happen to us, or we can actively choose and create the kind of life we want. This has always been our power. If we had forever to actualize our potentials, there would be no urgency about doing so. Our time is invaluable precisely because it is limited.

My Lifeline

Directions: On a separate sheet of paper, draw a horizontal line like the one above. Put a dot at the end of each line.

1. Over the left dot, put the number zero. This dot represents your birth. Write your birth date under this dot.

2. The dot on your right represents your ultimate death. How long do you think you'll live? At what age do you think you will die? (I recognize that this is not easy to think about.) Over the right dot, put a number that indicates your best guess as to how many years you think you will live. This guess should be based on present lifestyle (e.g. seatbelts, smoking, etc.) and family history. Write your estimated date of death under the right dot.

3. Now, place a dot that represents where you are right now on the line between birth and death. Write today's date under this dot.

This is your lifeline. Look at it, study it, and think about it. Let it settle into your consciousness.

A. On your lifeline, make note (marking approximate dates) of any significant experiences you have had up until this day.

B. In one paragraph, make note of those things that you are presently doing in your life that you find fulfilling and life affirming.

C. Map out what you plan to accomplish or what you think you would like to accomplish before you die.

AN ANALYSIS OF MY LIFE

1. Are you generally satisfied with what you have done so far in your life? Explain.

2. Have you accomplished more or less than you expected to for having reached this point in your life?

3. Are there any obstacles that you feel have interfered with your personal growth? If so what are they?

4. What, if anything, do you feel you can do to overcome these obstacles?

5. Who, or what, has had the greatest influence in helping you develop as a person?

6. If there was one thing that you could erase or subtract from your history, what would it be?

7. If there was one thing that you could add to your past, what would it be?

8. What is the most valuable lesson or piece of wisdom that you feel you have learned in life thus far?

9. If there was one thing that you could be guaranteed to accomplish before you died, what would it be?

10. If you accomplished all that you have planned for your future before you died, do you feel that you would be satisfied with your life?

11. Do you feel that you would be better able to accept your death?

12. Look at those goals that you have planned for your future. Are you presently doing something to actively pursue those goals? Explain.

13. Do you have a philosophy of life that you try to live by? Please share it here.

14. After you are gone, what would you like remembered about you? What would you like your epitaph to say?

15. As a result of this experience, I have learned...

I know that this was not an easy assignment to think about and I thank you for your effort.

---

* When giving this assignment to my students, I make it very clear that I have tremendous respect for the variety of faiths that any of them may practice, and the beliefs they may or may not embrace relative to an "afterlife." I further clarify that my reference to our being "finite" beings is made in regard to "this life" as we know it.

I also clarify, regarding my interpretation of Socrates, that when he states that "the truth lies within us and not in the stars, or in tradition, or in religious books," this again is not meant to be an affront to anyone's religious beliefs. Rather, I tell my students that I believe that Socrates is suggesting that no matter how often one attends a place of worship and listens to the sermons of one's minister, priest, or rabbi that ultimately the individual listening to such sermons will be the final filter as to how much of what is being said will be embraced, experienced, and lived. This explanation is an important one for both students and their parents who might otherwise be concerned that such an exercise in introspection might be in conflict with their faith.

CHAPTER TEN

THE PARABLE OF
THE BIRD IN THE HANDS

I end this book with one of my favorite stories about life and the will to choose and create one's destiny.

It seems that there is a wise man who lives at the top of a mountain, and every day, people troubled by their lives climb this mountain, seeking wisdom and guidance. When they return, they always do so with a smile and a look of tranquility in their eyes, having come to a deeper understanding and insight by way of the wise man's teaching.

A small boy of twelve resides at the base of this mountain, and finds himself jealous of this man's reputation and decides that he is going to be the first to outfox him. So he goes looking for a sparrow's nest, whereupon he removes a baby sparrow, and decides that he is going to climb the mountain with the bird cupped in his hands and then ask the wise man if the bird in his hands is alive or if it's dead. If the wise man says that it is dead, the boy is going to release it and let it fly. If the wise man says that it is alive, he is going to clench his hands and suffocate the bird.

Very excited with his plan, he climbs the mountain, and with the bird cupped in his hands he says, "Wise man. Can you tell me if the bird in my hands is alive or if it's dead?" The wise man looks at him and, gently smiling, simply says, "It's in your hands, son. It's in your hands."

CONCLUSION

I f you are a teacher, or contemplating becoming one, I applaud you for endeavoring into one of the noblest, if not the noblest, profession of all. I hope that in some small way, this book has invited you to reflect upon the importance of knowing yourself, and of recognizing the significance of the meaning that you attach to your professional identity, and the extremely invaluable work that you are doing in this world. I wish you all the joy that I have known in the classroom, and years filled with more of that to come. Please contact me if you'd like the dialogue to continue. I would relish in that opportunity.

John Perricone E-mail: KeynoteJP@aol.com

John Perricone's Bio

Mr. Perricone has been a health educator in the Maine-Endwell School District for twenty-two years. His love and passion for teaching have made him the recipient of local, state, and national "Excellence in Teaching" awards, and he has been the recipient of Maine-Endwell's Distinguished Teacher Award for seven consecutive years since its inception in 1997. This award is voted on and presented by the senior class.

In his book *Educating for Character*, Dr. Tom Lickona cites Mr. Perricone as a shining example of teaching at its best. He was the instructor of Hidy Ochiai's Karate of Cortland for sixteen years and in addition to teaching high school he is currently involved in training teachers throughout the state in the nationally recognized EKP (Educational Karate Program)—a character education program emphasizing non-violence, mental and physical fitness, and universal values of integrity, self-respect, and respect for others. After thirty-two years of training, Mr. Perricone recently received his 6th degree blackbelt—among the highest ranks that world-renowned Master Ochiai has ever awarded in his 37 years of teaching.

He sings with the Southerntiersmen Barbershop Chorus and performs throughout the state and beyond in a quartet known as the Troubadours. The only thing that exceeds his zest for his profession and hobbies are the love of his wife Vicki and his daughters Loren and Hannah.

APPENDIX

AN INTRODUCTION TO HEALTH EDUCATION
Instructor: Mr. J. Perricone

1. MY EXPECTATIONS: What I expect of my students is never kept secret. This paper is intended to make you aware of my expectations so that our time together will be productive and serene from our first to our last day. Please keep this for future reference.

It is my opinion that education need not be boring. By the same token, I am not, nor should I be expected to be Jim Carrey. What is important is that *you* take responsibility for your own learning. Those who fail to see their role in the learning process can easily blame the system to support a stance of helplessness. I have learned to have little sympathy with those who maintain an apathetic attitude toward their learning while doing nothing but complain about their boring teachers and their irrelevant classes. If you are dissatisfied with your education, I hope that you will look not only at the faults of "the system" but at yourself as well to see how much you are willing to do to make it vital. Are you just waiting for others to make your learning meaningful? How much are you willing to do to change those things that you don't like? Are you accepting your share of responsibility for putting something into the learning process?

I expect to give my very best to make this class interesting and stimulating, and therefore expect nothing less than your best efforts in return. Such effort includes excellent attendance, preparation for class, listening to and following directions, class participation, and completing assigned work on time. (Public affirmation.)

2. MATERIALS NEEDED EACH DAY: (Staying organized will really help you succeed.)

A. Assignment notebook (something to formally write your assignments in each day)
B. Health notebook
C. Assignment for the day (no excuses please)
D. Pen/pencil
E. Binder/folder for class handouts (portfolio turned in at end of semester)
F. Your mind and body ready to dance

3. WHAT ARE YOUR RIGHTS IN THIS CLASSROOM?
TO LEARN: As a student it is your right and privilege to learn without distraction. No one has the right to violate another person's right to learn, and such violations *will not* be tolerated. *Please* show consideration to others.

4. WHAT ARE MY RIGHTS AS INSTRUCTOR OF THIS COURSE?
TO TEACH: This is my job. I have earned my license to teach, and therefore no one has the right to violate my right to do my job. (I would assume that if your parents were surgeons you would not step into the operating room in the middle of their work and yell, "What's for supper?" Similarly, I ask that my work not be interrupted.)

For all the complaining that goes on about how much school stinks, I have found over the years that many enlightened people are interested in getting more than just a credit out of their classes, and it is out of respect for you that I will do everything that I can to uphold and protect your rights. Please remember at all times that this is your room and your class, and that the behavior of each person will shape the type of learning that will occur. Because one person's behavior affects everyone else, I respectfully request that everyone in the class, and not just me, be responsible for classroom management.

To insure that our rights are protected and upheld, the following laws have been established for this classroom:

The Law: To Be Followed Without Exception

1. Be on time, prepared, and ready to work from the beginning to the end of class. (Let me dismiss.)

2. Please raise your hand when you wish to speak and wait to be called upon.

3. Please listen to others with all your heart and soul. I will do the same.

4. Please treat others as you would like to be treated.

From our first day together I'll tell you that I love being a teacher and very much enjoy relating to people on a *mutual* respect level. It has been my experience that human interaction can be tremendously rewarding when such respect exists. I will always extend this consideration to you, and ask only that you return this in kind. Thank you. (Today is "clean slate day.")

OBJECTIVES
(What was I supposed to learn today?
What's he going to ask on the exam?)
When you come to class each day you will see the statement, "Today's objectives are numbers 1,2,3, etc." written on the board. These numbers will refer you to your objective sheet. Record these numbers in your notes and review the objectives before class. The objectives guide you as to what will be covered that day and what it is that I am asking you to be responsible for by the end of that day's lesson. All questions asked of you on any future exam will be derived from these objectives.

ASSIGNMENTS
(Self-reflection exercises, independent projects,
papers, interviews, etc.)
Assignments will always be written on the board below that day's objectives. *Please* write these in your assignment notebook before class begins. Unless I forget, I will always explain the assignment in

class. Unless you are told otherwise, the assignment will always be due on the day after it was assigned. *Late assignments* will receive *half credit* and will only be accepted within three days of their original due date. (Punctuality matters in the real world.) Please *do not* bring late assignments to me at the end of the year.

IF YOU ARE ABSENT
(This week in review, see me before homeroom/
after school, have a "buddy")

If you are absent, it is expected that you will make up assignments within the time allotted for legal absence. Please come in before homeroom or after school to obtain work missed and please don't ever—and I repeat *ever*—tell me that you didn't know that an assignment was due or that I didn't give it to you. Obtaining assignments missed is *your* responsibility. Capisce?

YOUR GRADE
(How do I get a good grade in this class?)

All assignments will receive a point value. At the end of each marking period, your grade will be determined by dividing the number of total points you have earned by the sum of the assignments' values. (You scored 230 of 250 possible points. Divide 230/250 = 92%.) Examinations account for only about 50% of your final average with assignments making up the rest. I have divided the course work in this way so that students who do not perform so well on exams can still earn a respectable grade. By the same token, individuals with 100 averages on exams who have not turned in any assignments can fail the course.

If at any time you need help, have a question, or would just like to talk—my door is open. I'm very much looking forward to our time together.

REFERENCES

Birch, L. (1984). Eating as the 'Means' Activity in a Contingency: Effects on Young Children's Food Preferences. CHILD DEVELOPMENT 55 (2,Apr: 431-439. EJ 303 231.

Koestenbaum, Peter. (1976) *Is There An Answer to Death?* Englewood Cliffs, N.J.: Prentice-Hall, 1976.

Kohn, A. (1993) *Punished by Rewards: The Trouble With Gold Stars, Incentive Plans, A's and Other Bribes.* Boston: Houghton Mifflin.

Lepper, M. (1973). *The Hidden Costs of Reward.* Hillsdale, NJ: Erlbaum

Printed in the United States
39901LVS00006B/190-516

9 781413 766486